Follo

God

Fruitful lives from the Bible

Following God

Fruitful lives from the Bible

Carine Mackenzie

CF4•K

10 9 8 7 6 5 4 3 2 1
© Copyright 2011 Carine Mackenzie
ISBN: 978-1-84550-750-3

Published in 2011 by
Christian Focus Publications,
Geanies House, Fearn, Tain
Ross-shire, IV20 1TW,
Great Britain

Cover design by Daniel van Straaten
Illustrations by Fred Apps
Printed and bound by Bell and Bain, Glasgow

The Scripture version used throughout this book is The King James or the author's own paraphrase.

But the fruit of the Spirit is love, joy, peace, long-suffering, gentleness, goodness, faith, meekness, temperance: against such there is no law.
Galatians 5:22–23

Ephesians 5:8– 10
...Walk as children of light: (For the fruit of the Spirit is in all goodness and righteousness and truth;) proving what is acceptable unto the Lord.

Written for
Lydia, Esther, Philip
Lois, Jack, Marianne, Isobel and Elizabeth

Contents

Look out for these logos throughout the book. See if you can remember what each logo stands for when you see it.

Right and Wrong

Fruit of the Spirit

Love

Joy

Peace

Long-suffering

Gentleness

Goodness

Faith

Meekness

Temperance

Jesus

When you see this logo there is a quiz for you to do!

Bible Search

Right and Wrong

• • • • • • • • • • • • • • • •

You might be asking yourself – why am I reading a book about fruit and fruitful lives? What does it mean to follow God? Well perhaps we should start with the question "What does it mean not to follow God?"

Have you watched the news on TV or perhaps the internet and seen the consequences of riots, vandalism, theft? You may have been astonished to witness the scenes in London and Birmingham as rioters looted shopping centres and burned businesses to the ground. Onlookers raised up their hands in horror. The one question that was on everyone's lips was 'Why?' A young Malaysian student was mugged as people walked by on the other side. He was physically hurt and his possessions were stolen. Nobody helped him. But people exclaimed 'How cruel!' when they saw it on the evening news. Others exclaimed, 'How evil!' when they saw families running for their lives from burning homes. Many thought it was 'greedy' when they saw others grab mobile phones and trainers in a mad illegal shop lifting spree.

These scenes that you see on the TV or hear about in the newspapers are examples of lives that do not follow God. Cruelty replaces kindness, evil replaces goodness, greed replaces self control. If you look up Galatians 5:22 you will read these words – Kindness, Goodness, Self Control – they are some of The fruit of the Spirit. These are the virtues and characteristics that mark someone out as belonging to God and a follower of his ways. The Fruit of the Spirit is something that is sadly absent from our towns and cities. So that's why we need to study this passage of scripture.

If you're not sure whether you are a Christian or not you need to look at this chapter of the Bible to see if the Holy Spirit is in your life and if your life is bearing fruit for God.

In our world today people do not know what is right and wrong because they are no longer exposed to the truth of God's Word. Be careful that you are not one of those who neglects God's word. Because then you will find that you are one of those people who is uncertain about what is the right way to behave. You will not know the difference between what is right and what is wrong. That is why this book and others like it need to be on the shelves of Christian families; in schools; libraries; youth centres. Better than that this book and the scripture it teaches need to be in the hands, minds and hearts of the young people and families who attend these schools and centres.

In this book, *Following God*, Bible characters are used to illustrate how we can see the Fruit of the Spirit in a person's life. Through people like the Good Samaritan who showed love, David who showed kindness and our Lord Jesus Christ who is the ultimate example of all these fruits or virtues – we see living and breathing examples of what is right and what is wrong.

One Fruit

• • • • • • • • • • • • • • • • • •

Paul, the great apostle and missionary wrote a letter to the churches in Galatia, part of the country we now call Turkey. Paul had set up those churches on his first missionary journey. He wanted to encourage them to keep following Christ and not to fall back into the old ways of sin and ritual. He points out the difference between a man living under the influence of sin and the man living under the influence of Christ. Their lives are totally different.

A life ruled by sin is full of hatred, strife, envy, impurity, anger, heresy. Such people do not inherit the kingdom of God. They are not trusting in Christ and their lives are not influenced by the Holy Spirit.

A life influenced by God, the Holy Spirit, is characterised by the fruit of the Spirit. Paul gives a list, not of different fruits of the Spirit, but of a variety of qualities found in the one fruit of the Spirit.

The fruit of the Spirit is:

Love, Joy, Peace, Patience, Kindness, Goodness, Faithfulness, Meekness, Temperance

We should be looking in our behaviour for evidence that the Spirit is working in our life and producing his fruit there. All these qualities make up the fruit. It is not enough for us to say, 'I am showing patience in my life, so I do not need to bother that I do not have kindness or love.'

The Christian character should show all aspects of the fruit of the Spirit. This is not something a person can work up by himself. The difference comes because Christ is in the believer by his Spirit. 'Christ in you, the hope of glory' (Colossians 1:27).

True Love

• • • • • • • • • • • • • • •

We have a big tree in the middle of our back garden. If you came to visit in September, you would recognise immediately that it was a plum tree because of the beautiful fruit that it bears. In winter time it is not so easy to identify, because the branches are bare, no fruit or leaves.

The Bible tells us that a Christian is known by his fruit. What kind of fruit could that be? Galatians chapter 5 gives a whole list of the fruit of the Spirit. The first on that list is LOVE.

Someone came to Jesus one day and asked him what was the greatest commandment. 'The greatest is to love the Lord God with all your heart, and soul and strength and mind,' Jesus replied. 'The second is to love your neighbour as yourself.' Jesus summed up the Ten Commandments with the word 'love' – love to God firstly and then love to the people we come in contact with.

Jesus told a story about the good Samaritan who put himself in danger and went to a great deal of trouble to help a poor man mugged on a lonely road. He showed true love to that man in need. Love is not just a feeling. True Christian love means action.

A beautiful description of Christian love is given in 1 Corinthians 13. If our lives are to show this fruit of love then the description of love (or charity) would fit us. Are we kind and long-suffering? Are we not envious? Are we modest, not wanting to push ourselves ahead of others? Do we behave wisely, put others first, refuse to take offence? Are our thoughts pure? Do we rejoice in what is true rather than what is evil? Do we put up with difficulties bravely? Do we believe the truth? Is our life one of hope and trust in God, enduring hardship for the sake of the Lord? That sort of behaviour is what God calls love. That is quite a list and how far short we fall of God's standard.

But one person lived a completely fruitful life every day in every way, the Lord Jesus Christ. He lived a life for us that we cannot live and he died for us too. Jesus was so kind, healing the sick and teaching the ignorant. Jesus lived humbly and simply. The Son of God did not push himself forward or take advantage of his true position. Jesus always behaved wisely, always spoke the truth, no evil word or thought ever came from him.

He endured so much, even to death on a cross and then the grave. The greatest display of love was his dying for his people on the cross. He not only died to pay the price for sin but rose again for our justification, to make us right with God. We love him because he first loved us. We show this love to God by worshipping him and by loving our neighbour, taking care of the hungry, needy and sick. 'Inasmuch as ye have done it unto the least of these my brethren, ye have done it unto me,' said Jesus. (Matthew 25:40)

If someone looked at your life, would they recognise love, the fruit of the Spirit in you?

Bible Search

Find the words missing from the verses. If your answers are correct, the initial letters will spell out a phrase connected to the story.

1. And let us consider one another to provoke unto love and to _____ works (Hebrews 10:24).

2. _____ rebuke is better than secret love (Proverbs 27:5).

3. Better is a _____ of herbs where love is, than a stalled ox and hatred therewith (Proverbs 15:17).

4. Love worketh no _____ to his neighbour: therefore love is the fulfilling of the law (Romans 13:10).

5. For God hath not given us the _____ of fear; but of power, and of love, and of a sound mind (2 Timothy 1:7).

6. Remembering without ceasing your work of faith, and

_____ of love, and patience of hope in our Lord Jesus Christ (1 Thessalonians 1:3).

7. He brought me to the banqueting house, and his banner _____ me was love (Song of Solomon 2:4).

8. Charity suffereth long, and is kind; charity envieth not; charity _____ not itself, is not puffed up (1 Corinthians 13:4).

9. But love ye your _____ and do good, and lend, hoping for nothing again; and your reward shall be great (Luke 6:35).

Real Joy

• • • • • • • • • • • • • • • • •

What makes you really happy? When do you feel joy? Perhaps if you are saving up to buy a special game, and when at last you are able to go to the shop to buy it, you might feel very happy. Or you may be looking forward to going on holiday. How glad you are when the day actually arrives and you set off. The joy you have from a game or a holiday does not last. Before long the game is broken or you don't find it so interesting any more. In a few days the holiday is over.

Real lasting joy only comes from God and the wonderful gifts he gives to his people. David in Psalm 37 tells us to 'delight in God and he will give us the desires of our heart'.

If we are truly delighting in God then the desires of our heart will be the things of God which God loves to give to his people. The gift of salvation gives us joy no matter what our circumstances may be.

Habakkuk could say, 'Yet I will rejoice in the LORD, I will joy in the God of my salvation' (Habakkuk 3:18), even if life was very difficult and he was in great suffering.

Our salvation comes through Jesus Christ and his death on the cross in our place. Paul said, 'We also joy in God through our Lord

Jesus Christ, by whom we have now received the atonement' (Romans 5:11). What joy to be at one with God, made possible only by the finished work of Christ.

When the Lord Jesus was born, the angel announced to some shepherds out watching their flocks at night, 'I bring you good tidings of great joy, which shall be to all people. For unto you is born this day in the city of David, a Saviour which is Christ the Lord' (Luke 2:10–11). When the wise men were guided by the star to the place where Jesus was, they rejoiced with exceeding joy (Matthew 2:10).

After Jesus died and was buried in the tomb, Mary Magdalene and another Mary went to see the tomb. An angel spoke to them. 'He is not here for he is risen' (Matthew 28:6). They ran off quickly to tell the disciples, feeling a bit afraid but also full of great joy. What marvellous news, Jesus had risen from the dead.

The disciples met with the risen Lord Jesus several times. He led them out to Bethany one day, blessed them and then ascended up through the clouds to heaven. The disciples returned to Jerusalem with great joy. The joy of the Lord was their strength. The men who had previously been scared and cowardly now became bold preachers of the gospel. God's Word gives us joy. Can you say what the Psalmist said in Psalm 119:14, 'I have rejoiced in the way of thy testimonies, as much as in all riches'? Going to the house of God should give us joy. David said, 'I was glad when they said unto me, let us go into the house of the LORD' (Psalm 122:1). Do you feel the same?

Sin can spoil our joy. If we are not delighting in God, or taken up with Jesus Christ, then we too easily fall into sin. David knew this very well. When he realised how greatly he had sinned against God, he begged for mercy and forgiveness. 'Restore unto me the joy of thy salvation,' he prayed (Psalm 51:12). 'Make me to hear joy and gladness; that the bones which thou hast broken may rejoice.' (Psalm 51:8). Sin had caused him to lose his joy but with God's sweet gift of repentance came the return of his joy.

Paul's prayer for the believers in Rome could be our prayer for ourselves and our family and friends.

'Now the God of hope, fill you with all joy and peace in believing, that ye may abound in hope, through the power of the Holy Ghost.' (Romans 15:13).

Bible Search

Find the words missing from the verses. The initial letters of your answers will spell out something from the story.

1. I have no _____ joy than to hear that my children walk in truth (3 John 4).

2. My mouth shall praise thee with joyful _____ (Psalm 63:5).

3. How that in a great trial of affliction the _____ of their joy and their deep poverty abounded unto the riches of their liberality (2 Corinthians 8:2).

4. Therefore with joy shall ye _____ water out of the wells of salvation (Isaiah 12:3).

5. Let them also that love thy _____ be joyful in thee (Psalm 5:11).

6. In thy presence is fullness of joy; at thy right hand there are pleasures for _____ (Psalm 16:11).

24

7. I will offer in his tabernacle _____ of joy; I will sing, yea, I will sing praises unto the LORD (Psalm 27:6).

8. Your _____ shall be turned into joy (John 16:20).

Peace for You

● ● ● ● ● ● ● ● ● ● ● ● ● ● ● ● ●

You only have to open a newspaper or listen to the news bulletin to learn of wars and fighting all over the world. In our own country there is violence on the streets and unrest and discord in many families. Politicians make long speeches describing their answer to the search for peace but they make very little difference. Discord and violence are a result of sin. The sinful human condition gives rise to putting ourselves before anyone else.

Jesus speaking to his disciples before his death, promised them peace but not the kind of peace that the politicians are looking for. 'My peace I give to you,' he said. 'Not as the world giveth give I unto you. Let not your heart be troubled, neither let it be afraid.' Jesus was speaking about the peace that a believer is given even when life is in a turmoil. Jesus reassured his disciples that he had come for them, and his gift for them was peace. In the world they would have trouble. Peter was thrown in prison. Stephen was stoned to death. Christians are still persecuted for their faith today, but the wonderful peace-giving news is that Jesus has overcome the world.

The peace which God gives is his own peace – not a man-made peace treaty which is so easily broken.

This peace passes all understanding. It keeps our hearts and minds focussed on Jesus Christ.

If we listen to God's commandments and obey his Word, God tells us our peace will be like a river (Isaiah 48:18). The source of the river is God himself. The river of peace flows through our lives giving refreshment and nourishment. A river flows out into the ocean and this river flows out into the ocean of God's eternal peace.

When we feel uneasy and our minds are full of anxious thoughts, what should we do? Think about the Lord and trust in him. 'Thou wilt keep him in

perfect peace, whose mind is stayed on thee: because he trusteth in thee' (Isaiah 26:3). What a marvellous promise to God's people. The LORD will bless his people with peace.

Peace is part of the fruit of the Spirit that should be evident in the life and conduct of the believer. Christ is our peace. He is the one who reconciles us to God, working out for us the great Peace Treaty that can never be broken and giving us the greatest peace imaginable – peace with God.

29

Bible Search

Find the missing words from the text. The initial letters of your answers will spell out the story topic.

1. For he is our peace, who hath made both one, and hath broken down the middle wall of _____ between us (Ephesians 2:14).

2. _____ to keep the unity of the Spirit in the bond of peace (Ephesians 4:3).

3. And came and preached peace to you which were _____ off and to them that were nigh (Ephesians 2:17).

4. ... the _____ of our peace was upon him; and with his stripes we are healed (Isaiah 53:5).

5. Then said Jesus to them again, 'Peace be unto you; as my Father hath sent me, _____ so send I you' (John 20:21).

6. And as many as _____ according to this rule, peace be on them and mercy, and upon the Israel of God (Galatians 6:16).

7. As for such as turn aside unto their crooked ways, the LORD shall lead them forth with the workers of iniquity; but peace shall be upon _____ (Psalm 125:5).

8. Therefore being justified by faith we have peace with God _____ our Lord Jesus Christ (Romans 5:1).

9. Thine are we, David, and on thy side, thou son of Jesse; peace, peace be unto thee and peace be to thine _____ ; for thy God helpeth thee (1 Chronicles 12:18).

10. And he said to the woman, Thy faith hath saved thee, _____ in peace (Luke 7:50).

11. Be perfect, be of good comfort, be of _____ mind, live in peace; and the God of love and peace shall be with you (2 Corinthians 13:11).

12. _____ from evil, and do good; seek peace and pursue it (Psalm 34:14)

Waiting Patiently

• • • • • • • • • • • • • • • • •

Have you ever planted seeds or bulbs in the garden? When you were very little you may have gone out the next day to see if the flowers had appeared. It takes time for the flowers to grow and we have to wait patiently until they push through the ground. The farmer plants the seed and has to wait patiently for the harvest time to come. It can sometimes feel like a long time to wait. That's why the Bible sometimes calls this 'long-suffering'.

God's people have to be patient too. 'Be patient,' James tells us, 'unto the coming of the Lord. Be patient: stablish your hearts: for the coming of the Lord draweth nigh.' God's timing is always right. He has promised that Jesus will return to the earth, but only God knows when and we must wait patiently.

It is appointed unto men once to die and only God knows the date of that appointment too. We must patiently believe and leave it all in God's hands.

Sometimes we can worry and fret when bad things are happening to us, but God tells us to be patient in tribulation (Romans 12:12). David in Psalm 37 tells us to rest in the LORD and wait patiently for him and not to fret when we see wicked people getting on better than us.

Following God

In our foolishness we can wish for something to happen and then do all we can to make sure that comes to pass. God's way is for us to seek him first and then all things will be added to us in his will. If we are patiently delighting in God, we will not lack any good thing for we will be perfectly satisfied with him.

How much better to be content with God than to be fretting for lesser things. When the troubles of life come our way, these can help us to learn patience. This patience gives us experience of God's dealings with us, which leads to hope in him because of his great love to us (see Romans 5:3–5).

Jesus rebuked Martha for being impatient with her sister, Mary. 'She has left me to do all the work alone. Tell her to help me,' she complained.

'Martha, Martha,' Jesus said, 'you are careful and troubled about many things.'

Jesus commended Mary for sitting beside him and listening to his teaching. Patiently resting and waiting on God is a much more important occupation than making the meal.

We should seek to lead our lives with patience, 'looking unto Jesus the author and finisher of our faith, who for the joy that was set before him endured the cross, despising the shame and is set down at the right hand of the throne of God.'

Considering Jesus and what he has done for us will keep us from being weary and fretful and impatient.

35

Bible Search

Find the missing words. The initial letters of your answers should spell out the subject of the story.

1. The patient in spirit is better than the _____ in spirit (Ecclesiastes 7:8).

2. If when ye do well, and suffer for it, ye take it patiently, this is _____ with God (1 Peter 2:20).

3. Rejoicing in hope, patient in _____, continuing instant in prayer (Romans 12:12).

4. I waited patiently for the LORD and he _____ unto me, and heard my cry (Psalm 40:1).

5. And so, after he (Abraham) had patiently _____ , he obtained the promise (Hebrews 6:15).

6. Be ye also patient; stablish your hearts: for the coming of the Lord draweth _____ (James 5:8).

7. For whatsoever things were written aforetime were written for our learning, that we through patience and _____ of the scriptures might have hope (Romans 15:4).

8. Preach the word; be instant in season, out of season; reprove, rebuke, _____ with all long-suffering and doctrine (2 Timothy 4:2).

Kindness

• • • • • • • • • • • • • • • • • •

We have a good friend who often helps us and many other people. With her sewing machine she makes T-shirts for Romanian orphans or alters a skirt that is too long for me. She bakes and cooks for old friends. She takes people in her car for hospital visits or to the shops. Her kindness gives pleasure and practical help to many people.

The Bible tells us that gentleness or kindness is part of the fruit of the Spirit. Giving to others – either time or material things without looking for something in return – is a grace given to the Christian by God.

David was the king of Israel, an important man. Jonathan, Saul's son, had been a great friend to him when Saul had been trying to kill David. After Saul and Jonathan had been killed in battle, David made enquiries. 'Is there any left of the house of Saul that I may show him kindness for Jonathan's sake?'

He was informed that Jonathan's son, Mephibosheth, was still living. He had been injured when the family were fleeing from danger and he was now lame. David sent for Mephibosheth. 'Don't be afraid,' he told him. 'I want to show you kindness for your father's sake.' David gave Mephibosheth

the land that had belonged to his grandfather, Saul, and servants to work the land for him. Mephibosheth was also allowed to sit at the king's table just like one of his sons.

Ruth showed great kindness to her mother-in-law, Naomi, going out to work in the fields to find food for the household. Dorcas showed great kindness to the widows and orphans in her town, making clothes for those in great need.

Joseph was kind to his brothers who had been unkind to him. He could have got his own back and punished them when they came looking for grain. But instead he gave them what they needed, even putting their money back in their sacks. Joseph knew that God was in the whole situation, working all things together for good.

The greatest act of kindness is from God. God the Father loved the world so much that he 'gave his only begotten Son that whosoever believeth on him should not perish but have everlasting life' (John 3:16). Such amazing kindness saves God's people from the punishment that their sin deserves.

The Lord Jesus Christ showed wonderful loving-kindness by willingly dying on the cross to take the punishment and curse to himself that is due to his followers. He gave so much. He gave himself.

Bible Search

Find the missing words. The initial letters of your answers will spell out the name of someone in the story.

1. Shew thy _____ loving-kindness (Psalm 17:7).

2. How _____ is thy loving-kindness O God! Therefore the children of men put their trust under the shadow of thy wings (Psalm 36:7).

3. They spake unto him, saying, If thou be kind to this _____ and please them and speak good words to them, they will be thy servants for ever (2 Chronicles 10:7).

4. Put on therefore as the elect of God, holy and beloved, bowels of mercies, kindness, _____ of mind, meekness, long-suffering. (Colossians 3:12).

5. He that hath two coats, let him _____ to him that hath none; and he that hath meat let him do likewise (Luke 3:11).

6. Because thy loving-kindness is _____ than life, my lips shall praise thee (Psalm 63:3).

7. And the maiden (Esther) pleased him (the king) and she _____ kindness of him; and he speedily gave her her things for purification (Esther 2:9).

8. Charity _____ long and is kind (1 Corinthians 13:4).

9. _____ my voice according unto thy loving-kindness (Psalm 119:149).

10. In a little wrath I hid my face from thee for a moment: but with _____ kindness will I have mercy on thee, saith the LORD thy Redeemer (Isaiah 54:8).

11. Be ye kind to one another, _____ forgiving one another, even as God for Christ's sake hath forgiven you (Ephesians 4:32).

12. Thou shalt not cut off thy kindness from my _____ for ever (1 Samuel 20:15).

Are You Really Good?

• • • • • • • • • • • • • •

Has anyone ever said to you, 'Are you a good boy today?' You probably replied, 'Yes!' Perhaps your Granny has said, 'What a good girl you are.' How pleased you would feel.

But are you really good? We can behave well on the outside, and people can think we are good, but what are we like on the inside? God looks on the heart. His Word tells us that the heart of man is deceitful above all things and desperately wicked. Jesus tells us that there is no one really good except God.

After God made the world, he looked at everything and said that it was good. Adam and Eve were good

in the Garden of Eden. They fell into sin by eating the forbidden fruit. They had rebelled against God and could no longer be called good. Every person born since then has been born a sinner.

By nature no one is able to consistently do good. 'There is none that doeth good, no, not one' (Romans 3:12). Very often when we want to do good things we find ourselves doing bad things that we don't want to do.

The Bible tells us that part of the fruit of the Spirit is goodness. How can we show goodness in our lives? Only through God, by his working in our lives to draw us to himself through the Lord Jesus Christ. 'He that doeth good is of God' (3 John 11). God's description of goodness is 'to do justly, and to love mercy and to walk humbly with thy God' (Micah 6:8).

God commands us to depart from evil and do good, by obeying his laws. Goodness comes from loving God because he first loved us. Goodness shows itself in many different ways: putting others before ourselves, helping the needy, giving generously, not envying, obeying God.

Barnabas was a good man (Acts 11:24). He trusted in God and was full of the Holy Spirit. His life showed kindness and helpfulness. He generously gave his property to the church. He preached God's message of salvation and was a great encouragement to God's people. His life was a fruitful life for God and all his good works came from God.

It is much easier to appear to be good on the outside. What about our thoughts? God asks us to think about things that are true and just, honest, pure and lovely (Philippians 4:8). We know that we often do or say or think things that are bad. Our only hope is to flee to the Lord Jesus Christ, to trust in his finished work and be covered with his goodness, the robe of his righteousness.

We will never be good enough on our own. But God in his rich mercy and grace is pleased to look on the goodness of his dear Son instead of our evil hearts.

As the hymn-writer said, 'The only fitness he requireth, is to know our need of him.'

Bible Search

Find the words missing from the verses. If your answers are correct, the initials will spell out the story subject.

1. They may by your good works which they shall behold, _____ God in the day of visitation (1 Peter 2:12).

2. The steps of a good man are _____ by the LORD: and he delighteth in his way (Psalm 37:23).

3. There is none good but _____ that is God (Matthew 19:17).

4. There was at Joppa a certain disciple ... called _____; this woman was full of good works and almsdeeds which she did (Acts 9:36).

5. As it is written there is _____ righteous, no, not one (Romans 3:10).

6. Your goodness is as a morning cloud and as the
_____ dew it goeth away (Hosea 6:4).

7. For he satisfieth the longing _____ and filleth
the hungry soul with goodness (Psalm 107:9).

8. But the _____ of the righteous is of
the LORD; he is their strength in the time of trouble
(Psalm 37:39).

Faith in God

• • • • • • • • • • • • • • • • • •

When you sat in the chair at breakfast-time today, did you expect it to hold you up safely? You probably did not even think about it. But you exercised faith or trust in the chair. If the chair had a broken leg you would have perhaps fallen to the floor. Your faith in the chair would have been misplaced, placed on something that was not dependable. What is really important is to place our faith on something that is good and dependable, and will not disappoint us.

The Bible tells us that without faith it is impossible to please God (Hebrews 11:6). Where is our faith to be placed? Only in the Lord Jesus Christ. He is the one who demonstrated who he is by suffering for our sin at Calvary and rising again. We must look to Jesus 'the author and finisher of our faith; who for the joy that was set before him, endured the cross, despising the shame, and is set down at the right hand of the throne of God' (Hebrews 12:2).

Jesus is totally dependable. He does not lie; he keeps all his promises; he has power to save us and keep us. We must rest in him alone for the salvation that he offers to us in the Gospel.

We need to have faith in Christ Jesus when we first believe. But we need that faith in him day by day to help us deal with problems. It was faith in God that helped David face up to Goliath.

We need faith to help us say, 'No' to sin. Joseph's faith in God helped him to turn away and run from the temptation of Potiphar's wife. Hebrews chapter 11 gives us a whole list of heroes of faith who did amazing things with God's help.

Jesus spoke about his followers having faith just like a grain of mustard seed, which is very tiny, but grows into a tree big enough for birds to nest in. Someone once said to a godly lady, 'You are a woman of great faith.' 'No,' she replied, 'I am a woman of little faith in a great God.'

It is vital that our faith, no matter how little or weak, is placed in the right person – the Lord Jesus Christ.

Faith can be summed up by this acrostic.

Forsaking

All

I

Trust

Him

We must believe what Jesus says to us in his Word the Bible and act on it in obedience. Faith is not something we can work up ourselves. It is a gift from God, a saving grace, part of the fruit of the Spirit. God is faithful to us. We should have faith in him.

Bible Search

Find the missing words. The initials of your answers will spell out something from the story.

1. _____ both to the Jews and also to the Greeks, repentance toward God, and faith toward our Lord Jesus Christ (Acts 20:21).

2. _____ without ceasing your work of faith, and labour of love, and patience of hope in our Lord Jesus Christ ... (1 Thessalonians 1:3).

3. For what if some did not believe? Shall their _____ make the faith of God without effect? God forbid (Romans 3:3–4).

4. Now faith is the _____ of things hoped for, the evidence of things not seen (Hebrews 11:1).

5. That ye stand fast in one spirit, with one mind striving _____ for the faith of the gospel (Philippians 1:27).

6. But without faith it is _____ to please him (Hebrews 11:6).

7. Neither is there salvation in any other: for there is none other _____ under heaven given among men, whereby we must be saved (Acts 4:12).

8. Jesus said to them, 'Verily, I say unto you, I have not found so _____ faith, no, not in Israel' (Matthew 8:10).

9. By whom we have received grace and apostleship, for _____ to the faith among all nations for his name (Romans 1:5).

10. Above all, taking the shield of faith, wherewith we shall be able to quench all the fiery _____ of the wicked (Ephesians 6:16).

Meekness not Weakness

● ● ● ● ● ● ● ● ● ● ● ● ● ● ● ● ● ●

When a grown-up asks you to put your toys away tidily, do you do it quickly and gently or do you roughly throw them into the toy-box complaining noisily? Do you treat your friends with courtesy and respect? Do you speak with gentle words instead of being rude and angry?

The Bible speaks about the gracious gift of the Holy Spirit called meekness. This word is not the same as servile weakness, it is in fact just the opposite, showing great inner strength given by God.

Meekness is first and foremost submitting to God's will, putting God before ourselves. 'Humble yourselves under the mighty hand of God,' Peter writes to the church (1 Peter 5:6). A meek spirit will be shown in how we deal with others, gentle and humble in obeying our parents and teachers, courteous and considerate with our brother and sister and friend. Even a simple thing like saying 'Please' or 'Thank you' will show meekness.

Moses is well known as a meek man, more meek than any other man living at that time. When his brother, Aaron, and sister, Miriam, spoke against Moses, he did not retaliate angrily. He left God to deal with them. When God punished Miriam for her rebellion by the disease of leprosy, Moses prayed earnestly to God for her recovery.

Stephen did not retaliate when the crowd was stoning him. He prayed that the Lord would forgive his attackers. What an amazing spirit of meekness given to him by God. A meek and quiet spirit is described as an ornament which is of great value to God, much more beautiful than any jewellery.

The greatest example of meekness is the Lord Jesus Christ himself. 'I am meek and lowly in heart,' he says as he invites troubled sinners to come to himself to find rest. His submission to his Father's will as he approached his suffering for sinners on the cross is the supreme example of meekness. He said, 'Not my will but thine be done' (Luke 22:42). All through his life he showed meekness. He did not retaliate or complain, 'Who when he was reviled, reviled not again; when he suffered, he threatened not; but committed himself to him that judgeth righteously' (1 Peter 2:23).

Jesus showed such consideration and gentleness in his dealing with people, the woman of Samaria, Zacchaeus and many others.

God has promised many blessings to those who display meekness, the fruit of the Spirit. 'God will beautify the meek with salvation '(Psalm 149:4). 'The meek will he guide in judgement and the meek will he teach in his way' (Psalm 25:9). 'The meek will inherit the earth' (Matthew 5:5).

The world may look on meekness as being weak and ineffective but actually meekness is the source of true happiness. 'The meek shall inherit the earth and shall delight themselves in the abundance of peace' (Psalm 37:11).

Bible Search

Find the missing words. The initials of your answers will spell out the names of two people in the story.

1. The LORD lifteth up the _____: he casteth the wicked down to the ground (Psalm 147:6).

2. Brethren, if a man be _____ in a fault, ye which are spiritual, restore such an one in the spirit of meekness ... (Galatians 6:1).

3. _____ ye the LORD, all ye meek of the earth, which have wrought his judgement (Zephaniah 2:3).

4. Blessed are the meek: for they shall inherit the _____ (Matthew 5:5).

5. The meek shall eat and be _____ (Psalm 22:26).

6. To speak evil of no man, to be no brawlers, but gentle, _____ all meekness unto all men (Titus 3:2).

7. The Spirit of the Lord God is upon me: because the Lord hath anointed me to preach good _____ unto the meek ... (Isaiah 61:1).

8. Lay apart all filthiness and superfluity of naughtiness and receive with meekness the _____ word, which is able to save your souls (James 1:21).

9. Follow after righteousness, godliness, faith, love, _____ , meekness (1 Timothy 6:11).

10. And Mary said, Behold the _____ of the Lord; be it unto me according to thy word (Luke 1:38).

11. Be ye all of one mind, having compassion one of another, love as brethren, be pitiful, be courteous, not rendering _____ for evil (1 Peter 3:8 & 9).

12. Father if thou be willing, remove this cup from me: _____ not my will, but thine, be done (Luke 22:42).

A Life Under Control

● ● ● ● ● ● ● ● ● ● ● ● ● ●

Have you ever watched a great athlete running a race or playing a hard game of rugby? The athlete only achieves peak fitness by training hard for months, denying himself certain foods and late nights. He must exercise strict discipline. The training and discipline enables him to get his body under control to perform well on the track or field.

The Christian life is like running a race, not to win a gold medal but the far more wonderful prize of an imperishable crown in heaven. 'Every man that striveth for the mastery is temperate in all things' (1 Corinthians 9:25). Temperance is part of the fruit of the Spirit.

Following God

Sometimes it is called self-control but we cannot control ourselves in our own strength. We need the help of God to live a disciplined and controlled life. The temperate life is controlled by Jesus. We must run the race with patience, looking to Jesus, the author and finisher of our faith. Jesus is the supreme example of a disciplined, temperate life. He endured the cross, despising its shame. He always spoke and acted wisely.

If our thoughts are to be temperate, we should think about Jesus. Our actions will be disciplined if we use our time to serve him. We learn how to think about him and serve him by reading his Word. Instead of reacting with irritation straightaway

when someone insults him, the wise man will keep his feelings hidden and not lose his temper.

If we are over-anxious about some problem, we are forgetting to cast all our cares on God. He asks us to commit every worry to him in prayer with thanksgiving. Even our grief should be temperate, as we remember that everything is in the control of a loving heavenly Father and he does all things well. All things work together for good to those who love God, who are the called according to his purpose.

The only way to live a temperate disciplined life is through Christ Jesus. 'I can do all things through Christ who strengtheneth me,' said Paul (Philippians 4:13).

'Without me, ye can do nothing,' Jesus tells us.

Bible Search

Find the missing words. The initial letters of your answers will spell out the story topic.

1. _____ let us not sleep, as do others; but let us watch and be sober (1 Thessalonians 5:6).

2. Be careful for nothing; but in _____ thing by prayer and supplication with thanksgiving let your requests be made known unto God (Philippians 4:6).

3. Let your _____ be known unto all men (Philippians 4:5).

4. (Add) to knowledge temperance; and to temperance _____; and to patience godliness (2 Peter 1:6).

5. Cease from anger and forsake wrath; fret not thyself in any wise to do _____ (Psalm 37:8).

6. And as he (Paul) _____ of righteousness, temperance and judgement to come, Felix trembled (Acts 24:25).

7. That the _____ men be sober, grave, temperate, sound in faith, in charity, in patience (Titus 2:2).

8. But put ye on the Lord Jesus Christ, and make _____ provision for the flesh, to fulfil the lusts thereof (Romans 13:14).

9. See that ye walk _____, not as fools, but as wise (Ephesians 5:15).

10. Wherefore gird up the loins of your mind, be sober, and hope to the _____ for the grace that is to be brought unto you at the revelation of Jesus Christ (1 Peter 1:13).

Jesus – The Perfect Example

• • • • • • • • • • • • • • • • •

Jesus Christ is the only one who displayed the fruit of the Spirit fully. He lived a perfect life for us.

He displayed LOVE when he laid down his life for his people. 'Greater love has no man than this, that a man lay down his life for his friends' (John 15:13).

'God commendeth his love toward us, in that, while we were yet sinners, Christ died for us' (Romans 5:8).

Jesus experienced true JOY in doing his Father's will and pleasing him. He wanted his followers to share in his joy. 'As the Father has loved me,' he said, 'so have I loved you; continue in my love. If you keep my commandment, you shall abide in my love; even as I have kept my Father's commandments, and abide in his love. These things I have spoken unto you, that my JOY might remain in you, and that your joy might be full' (John 15:9–11).

Jesus quietened troubled hearts and drove away fear, promising his people peace in their hearts, his own PEACE. 'Peace I leave with you, my PEACE I give unto you; not as the world gives, give I unto you. Let not your heart be troubled, neither let it be afraid' (John 14:27).

Jesus showed amazing PATIENCE as his enemies falsely accused him and he did not answer back. 'When he was accused of the chief priests and elders, he answered nothing' (Matthew 27:12). Isaiah had foretold the patience of the Lord Jesus. 'He was oppressed and he was afflicted, yet he opened not his mouth' (Isaiah 53:7).

We can see Jesus' KINDNESS in many ways, he fed the hungry, healed the sick, gave sight to the blind and called little children to come to him. 'Come unto me all ye that labour and are heavy laden, and I will give you rest' (Matthew 11:28).

Jesus' whole life was full of GOODNESS. He had no sin at all. Everything he did and said was good. 'He went about doing good, and healing all that were oppressed of the devil; for God was with him' (Acts 10:38).

Who is the greatest believer of all? – the Lord Jesus Christ. He believed God's Word and trusted in his Father. He had FAITH that God would accept his sacrifice on the cross for sinners. 'Who for the joy that was set before him, endured the cross, despising the shame and is set down at the right hand of the throne of God' (Hebrews 12:2).

Jesus showed MEEKNESS as he submitted to the will of his Father, and as he did not retaliate to those who insulted him. 'Who, when he was reviled, reviled not again; when he suffered, he threatened not; but committed himself to him that judgeth righteously' (1 Peter 2:23).

TEMPERANCE or discipline was evident in Christ's life. His prayer life was disciplined. 'And in the morning, rising up a great while before day, he went out and departed into a solitary place, and there prayed' (Mark 1:35). His whole life was disciplined so that he would fulfil his Father's will for the salvation of sinners. 'When the time was come ... he steadfastly set his face to go to Jerusalem' (Luke 9:51).

In a letter to the church at Ephesus, Paul says the fruit of the Spirit is goodness and righteousness and truth. These characteristics describe the Lord Jesus. We can only claim them as Christ lives in us, and we live in him.

Bible Search

Find the missing words. The initials spell out two words from the story.

1. And now abideth _____ , hope, charity, these three; but the greatest of these is charity (1 Corinthians 13:13).

2. For the fruit of the Spirit is in all goodness and _____ and truth (Ephesians 5:9).

3. He that walketh in his _____ feareth the LORD; but he that is perverse in his ways despiseth him (Proverbs 14:2).

4. All scripture is given by inspiration of God, and is profitable for doctrine, for reproof, for correction, for _____ in righteousness (2 Timothy 3:16).

5. And let the peace of God rule in your hearts, to the which also ye are called in one body; and be ye _____ (Colossians 3:15).

6. Grace be with all them that love our Lord Jesus Christ in _____ (Ephesians 6:24).

7. Praying always with all prayer and supplication in the Spirit, and watching thereunto with all _____ and supplication for all saints (Ephesians 6:18).

8. But without faith it is _____ to please him [God] (Hebrews 11:6).

9. Bring forth therefore fruits meet for _____ (Matthew 3:8).

10. That ye might walk worthy of the Lord unto all pleasing, being fruitful in every good work, and _____ in the knowledge of God (Colossians 1:10).

11. The fear of man bringeth a snare; but whoso putteth his _____ in the LORD shall be safe (Proverbs 29:25).

Answers

Quiz 1/Page 18

1. Good
2. Open
3. Dinner
4. Ill
5. Spirit
6. Labour
7. Over
8. Vaunteth
9. Enemies

Break the code: God is love

Quiz 2/Page 24

1. Greater
2. Lips
3. Abundance
4. Draw
5. Name
6. Evermore
7. Sacrifices
8. Sorrow

Break the code: Gladness

Quiz 3/Page 30

1. Partition
2. Endeavouring
3. Afar
4. Chastisement
5. Even
6. Walk
7. Israel
8. Through
9. Helpers
10. Go
11. One
12. Depart

Break the code: Peace with God

Quiz 4/Page 36

1. Proud
2. Acceptable
3. Tribulation
4. Inclined
5. Endured
6. Nigh
7. Comfort
8. Exhort

Break the code: Patience

1. Marvellous
2. Excellent
3. People
4. Humbleness
5. Impart
6. Better
7. Obtained
8. Suffereth
9. Hear
10. Everlasting
11. Tenderhearted
12. House

Break the code: Mephibosheth

Quiz 6/ Page 48

1. Glorify

2. Ordered

3. One

4. Dorcas

5. None

6. Early

7. Soul

8. Salvation

Break the code: Goodness

Quiz 7/ Page 54

1. Testifying

2. Remembering

3. Unbelief

4. Substance

5. Together

6. Impossible

7. Name

8. Great

9. Obedience

10. Darts

Break the code: Trust in God

Quiz 8/ Page 60

1. Meek
2. Overtaken
3. Seek
4. Earth
5. Satisfied
6. Shewing
7. Tidings
8. Engrafted
9. Patience
10. Handmaid
11. Evil
12. Neverthless
Break the code: Moses, Stephen

Quiz 9/ Page 66
1. Therefore
2. Every
3. Moderation
4. Patience
5. Evil
6. Reasoned
7. Aged
8. Not
9. Circumspectly
10. End
Break the code: Temperance

Quiz 10/ Page 72
1. Faith
2. Righteousness
3. Uprightness
4. Instruction
5. Thankful
6. Sincerity
7. Perseverance
8. Impossible
9. Repentance
10. Increasing
11. Trust
Break the code: Fruit, Spirit

Scripture Index
Old Testament

The following scriptures are referred to within the particular chapters

Genesis – Are You Really Good?

Exodus – Meekness not Weakness

Ruth – Kindness

1 Samuel – Faith in God

2 Samuel – Kindness

Psalms

Psalm 25:9 – Meekness not Weakness

Psalm 37 – Waiting Patiently

Psalm 37:11 – Meekness not Weakness

Psalm 51:8 – Real Joy

Psalm 51:12 – Real Joy

Psalm 119:14 – Real Joy

Psalm 122:1 – Real Joy

Psalm 149:4 – Meekness not Weakness

Isaiah 26:3 – Peace for You

Isaiah 48:18 – Peace for You

Micah 6:8 – Are You Really Good?

Habakkuk 3:18 – Real Joy

Scripture Index

New Testament

The following scriptures are referred to within the particular chapters

Extra Quiz

Fill in the blanks.

This I say then, Walk in the _ _ _ _ _ _, and ye shall not fulfil the lust of the flesh.

For the flesh lusteth against the _ _ _ _ _ _, and the _ _ _ _ _ _against the flesh: and these are contrary the one to the other: so that ye cannot do the things that ye would.

But if ye be led of the _ _ _ _ _ _, ye are not under the law.

Now the works of the flesh are manifest, which are these; _ _ _ _ _ _ _ _, fornication, uncleanness, lasciviousness, idolatry, _ _ _ _ _ _ _ _ _ _, hatred, variance, emulations, wrath, _ _ _ _ _ _, seditions, heresies, envyings, murders, _ _ _ _ _ _ _ _ _ _ _, revellings, and such like: of the which I tell you before, as I have also told you in time past, that they which do such things shall not inherit the kingdom of God. But the _ _ _ _ _of the _ _ _ _ _ _ is

_ _ _ _,   _ _ _,   _ _ _ _ _

_ _ _ _ _ _ _ _ _ _ _ _ _,   _ _ _ _ _ _ _ _ _ _

_ _ _ _ _ _ _ _,   _ _ _ _ _

_ _ _ _ _ _ _ _,   _ _ _ _ _ _ _ _ _ _: against such there is no law.

And they that are _ _ _ _ _ _'_ have crucified the flesh with the affections and lusts.

If we live in the _ _ _ _ _ _, let us also walk in the _ _ _ _ _ _.

Let us not be desirous of vain glory, provoking one another, envying one another.

Galatians 5:16– 26

Put the following words in the blanks. Turn to page 86 for the correct answer.

Spirit (7 times), Adultery; Drunkenness; Fruit; Joy; Goodness; Gentleness; Faith; Witchcraft; Strife; Love; Long-suffering; Peace; Meekness; Christ's; Temperance

Galatians 5: 16– 26

This I say then, Walk in the Spirit, and ye shall not fulfil the lust of the flesh.

For the flesh lusteth against the Spirit, and the Spirit against the flesh: and these are contrary the one to the other: so that ye cannot do the things that ye would.

But if ye be led of the Spirit, ye are not under the law.

Now the works of the flesh are manifest, which are these; Adultery, fornication, uncleanness, lasciviousness, idolatry, witchcraft, hatred, variance, emulations, wrath, strife, seditions, heresies, envyings, murders, drunkenness, revellings, and such like: of the which I tell you before, as I have also told you in time past, that they which do such things shall not inherit the kingdom of God.

But the fruit of the Spirit is love, joy, peace, long-suffering, gentleness, goodness, faith, meekness, temperance: against such there is no law.

And they that are Christ's have crucified the flesh with the affections and lusts.

If we live in the Spirit, let us also walk in the Spirit.

Let us not be desirous of vain glory, provoking one another, envying one another.

The Author

Carine Mackenzie has written over one hundred and fifty books for children. She has a talent for retelling Bible stories that has meant that children from all over the world have been given the opportunity to discover Jesus Christ for themselves.

Carine's writing started when she and her husband saw a need for children's books that retold Bible stories accurately. They had three young daughters who loved stories. Carine and her husband longed for them to come to know the Saviour who died for them on the cross. They also wanted their children to apply the truth of the Bible to their own lives.

So one day in the kitchen of her house in Inverness Carine sat down to write her first two books – Gideon the Soldier of God and Mary the Mother of Jesus.

Her 150th book was published in 2011 – 365 Great Bible Stories: The Good News of Jesus Christ from Genesis to Revelation.

With sales of over 3 million books world wide Carine continues to write books for children. It's not just her children who inspire her now to write books but her young grandchildren who love stories just as much as the previous generation.

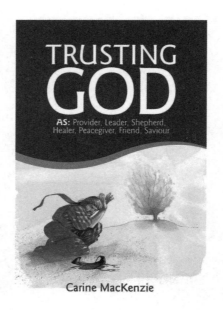

Carine MacKenzie

Do you know what your name means? Each year, a
list is compiled of the popular names given to babies
born in that year. The list changes slightly year on
year. God has many names that are truly unique.

Carine Mackenzie has taken seven of God's
names to explain them for children aged 7-11 years.
Using a Bible story, she shows them how these
names of God are still relevant to us today. Your
children will be fascinated by these new words.

ISBN: 978-1-84550-271-3

How to
handle
your life...
Carine
Mackenzie

Encouraging children to start a daily habit of Bible reading, prayer and meditation is important. Carine Mackenzie, an established children's Christian author, has compiled this collection of stories from her own life. Appropriate Bible passages are suggested for daily reading and prayer points are suggested.

The book is also illustrated with some appropriate black and white illustrations. It is an excellent devotional tool for 7 to 11 years old, as well as holding great potential for children's talks and assemblies. The puzzle feature really sets this book apart from the others and will give an extra dimension to a child's devotional life. The stories are divided into four sections: The Bible; Jesus; Life and our Father God.

ISBN: 978-1-85792-520-3

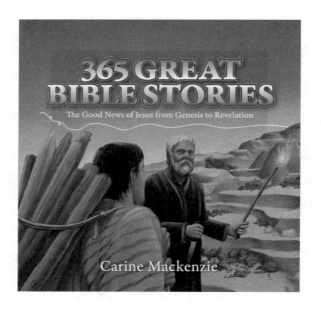

Carine Mackenzie's 150th Book. With one story a day this book will give you enough Bible stories to last all year. There is also an opportunity to track a theme such as Salvation; The Holy Spirit; God's Word and by looking out for the key picture as you flick through the book. Be sure to remember that this book is not about how fast or slow you read, or how many days you spend going through it. This book is about discovering the good news about Jesus Christ from Genesis to Revelation. You can also make a special friend, Jesus Christ, the true Saviour. He is with his people always no matter what time of day or what month of the year it is. God's word is true always. Read it and learn from it and follow it all the days of your life.

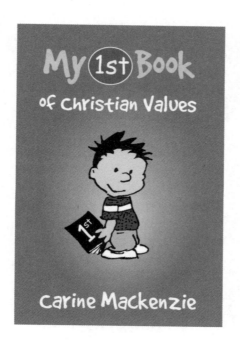

Are you full of questions? Do you need answers? Most children are just like you. This book will help. As well as having an amazing mind you have a soul that needs direction and care. With the work of the Holy Spirit the Christian principles and values from God's word, that are explained in this book, will be eternal and life changing.

In this book are thirty one different values that show us what Jesus Christ is like and how we should behave. Each value has a scripture verse to learn and a brief explanation.

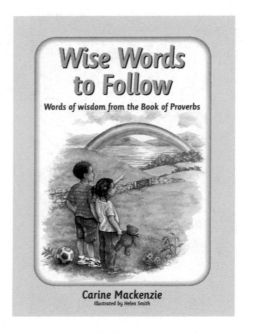

Wise Words to Follow

Words of wisdom from the Book of Proverbs

Carine Mackenzie
Illustrated by Helen Smith

Wise Words to Trust; Follow and Obey are three books by Carine Mackenzie to help you through the book of Proverbs. When you have problems you need someone to help you. You can't sort out your problems on your own. God is the best person to help you at anytime and in anyplace. He has given you a book full of wise words to follow. These words will help you to live a full and happy life.

Some of these helpful sayings are collected in this beautifully illustrated series of books and best-selling author, Carine Mackenzie, has added a few words of her own to help you understand what God wants you to do with your life.

Investigate the truth and open the Jesus files. Let the Bible present its case and uncover files of information that will help you research the real events, find out the most important discovery in history. Fact Files and Bible Data, Focus and Character studies are there to help you in your task.

This is an excellent Bible story book for the child or young person who needs to read a bible story book that is that little bit more sophisticated.